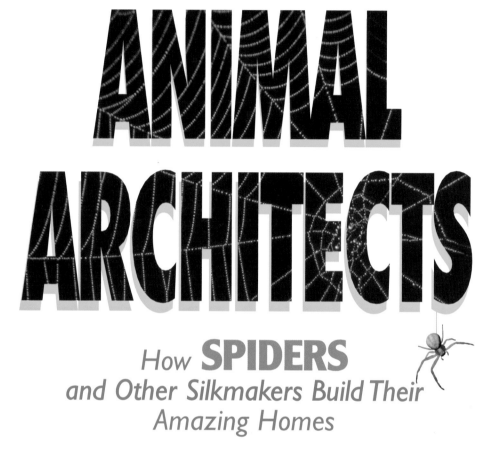

ANIMAL ARCHITECTS

How **SPIDERS**
and Other Silkmakers Build Their
Amazing Homes

W. Wright Robinson

BLACKBIRCH PRESS, INC.

WOODBRIDGE, CONNECTICUT

Acknowledgement
The author thanks Dr. Michael H. Robinson, Dr. F.A. Coyle, Dr. Vincent G. Dethier, and
Dr. J.A. Coddington for their help in reviewing all or part of the material for this book.

Dedication
To all children. Have the wisdom to sort out the meaningless hype that invades your
senses and learn to appreciate the beauty of the natural world, wherever you may be.

Published by Blackbirch Press, Inc.
260 Amity Road
Woodbridge, CT 06525

©1999 by Blackbirch Press, Inc.
First Edition

e-mail: staff@blackbirch.com
Web site: www.blackbirch.com

Printed in Hong Kong

10 9 8 7 6 5 4 3 2 1

Library of Congress Cataloging-in-Publication Data
Robinson, W. Wright.
    How spiders, caterpillars, and other silkmakers build their amazing homes / W. Wright
Robinson. — 1st ed.
        p.   cm. — (Animal Architects)
    Summary: Describes how spiders, caterpillars, and other creatures produce silk and use it
to make webs, tents, traps, and homes both above and below ground.
    Includes bibliographical references and index.
    ISBN 1-56711-378-8 (library binding : alk. paper)
    1. Spiders—Juvenile literature. 2. Caterpillars—Juvenile literature. 3. Animals'—
Habitations—Juvenile literature. [1. Spiders. 2. Caterpillars. 3. Animals—Habitations.]
I. Title. II. Series.
QL458. 4. R645   1999   98-52800
595.4'4—dc21   CIP
                                                                                AC

Contents

Introduction

The dictionary describes an architect as "a person whose profession is to design buildings and direct their construction." But people are not the only architects in the world! Human architects are at the end of a long line of remarkable builders. We are actually the most recent builders on the planet. Millions of years before the first human built the first building, animals were building their homes. Some even built large "cities."

Animal architects do not build from drawings or blueprints. Rather, they build from plans that exist only in their brains. Their building plans have been passed from parent to offspring over the course of millions of years.

Meet the Animal Architects

This book will introduce you to just a few of the many fascinating animal architects in the world today. You will discover how they design both resting and living spaces, cradles in which to raise their young, and places to gather and store their food. Most important, you will see how their buildings help them survive in the natural world.

Each group of animals has its own unique methods of construction. Clams, snails, and a few of their relatives build some of the most beautiful structures in all of nature. Their empty homes are the seashells you find at the beach.

Bees, ants, termites, and wasps are among the most interesting architects in the world of insects. They work alone or in large groups to build some remarkably complex homes. Some nests grow larger than a grocery bag and can include five or six stories, with entrances and exits throughout.

Spiders are magnificent architects whose small, often hard-to-find silk homes are every inch as complex and amazing as the larger homes of birds and mammals. Some spiders actually build trapdoors to hide themselves and ambush prey. Others construct beautiful square silken boxes as traps, while they hang suspended in the air!

Birds are another group of remarkable architects. Most people think a bird's nest is simply made of sticks and grass in the shape of a bowl. While this shape describes some nests, it by no means describes them all. Some, like the edible saliva nests of the swiftlets, for example, are quite unusual. In fact, our human ancestors may have learned to weave, sew, and make clay pots from watching winged architects build their nests!

The constructions of mammals are some of the grandest on Earth. Mammals are thinking animals. They can learn from their experiences and mistakes. Each time one of these animals builds a new home, it may be constructed a little differently, a little faster, and a little better.

I hope that you will enjoy reading these books. I also hope that, from them, you will learn to appreciate and respect the incredible builders of the animal world—they are the architects from whom we have learned a great deal about design and construction. They are also the architects who will continue to inspire and enlighten countless generations still to come.

W. Wright Robinson

Meet the Silkmakers

Silkmakers are some of the most remarkable animal architects. They make and use thin strands of a very strong but delicate material to build homes, traps, and cocoons. Some silkmakers are part of a group called arachnids, which includes all spiders, scorpions, mites, and ticks (though ticks are not silkmakers). Several kinds of centipedes and millipedes—part of another group—are also silkmakers.

A few insects, such as caterpillars and caddis fly larvae produce silk as well.

Unfortunately, the most crafty silkmakers are among the most overlooked and ignored builders in the world. There are most likely two reasons for this. First, spiders, the master silk builders, scare many people. Because of this, most people do not take the time or interest to look closely at the work that spiders do. The second reason is that silkmakers often build their homes in hard-to-find, out-of-the-way places. If you don't know where to look—or how to look—you will not see many of the most beautiful silk structures that these creatures create.

Almost anywhere you go, spiders and insects are a part of your world. Even though these animals are small and often move among us unseen, they deserve recognition as magnificent architects.

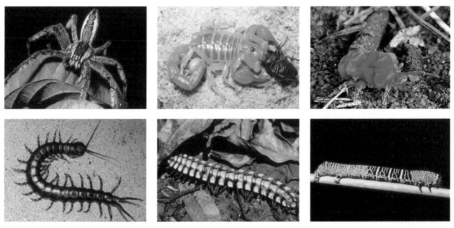

Notable silkmakers include (top row from left to right) spiders, scorpions, mites, (second row from left to right) centipedes, millipedes, and caterpillars. Caddisflies (right) produce silk while they are larvae.

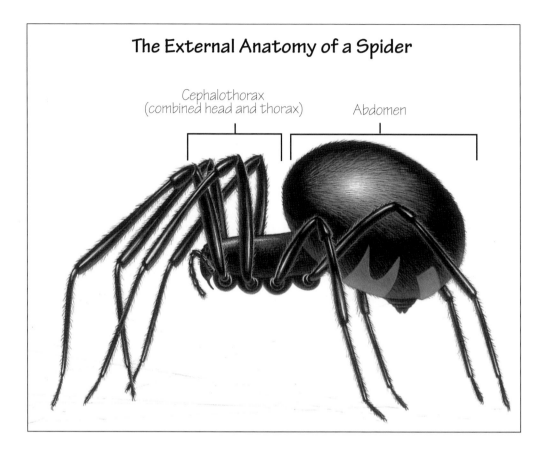

The External Anatomy of a Spider

Cephalothorax
(combined head and thorax)

Abdomen

Why a Spider Is Not an Insect

All insects share certain characteristics. Their bodies are made up of three parts: the head, thorax (chest), and abdomen (rear). A single pair of antennae (feelers) are found on the head. Insects have six legs, three on each side of the thorax. If the insect can fly, its wings are attached to this middle body part.

A spider is not an insect because it does not have these characteristics. A spider has only two body parts: a combined head and thorax, and an abdomen. Spiders have eight legs and no antennae.

What Do They Use Silk For?

Spiders are the best-known silkmakers in the world. Silk is so important to them that most spiders could not survive without it. These animals use their silk for such things as traveling, building homes, trapping food, and protecting their young.

Scorpions and mites use silk only to cover their fragile eggs. The strong silk wrapping helps protect the eggs from damage or destruction.

The silk produced by centipedes and millipedes may be used after mating. When their eggs are laid, some of these animals use silk to cover the eggs and give them extra protection. A few different kinds of millipedes work a little harder and make small silk nests to hold their eggs until they hatch.

Beautiful moths and butterflies emerge from caterpillars' silk encasings. During the early stage of its life, the insect wraps itself in silk. This fine silk covering is called a cocoon. It helps protect the young animal from harm while its body is changing and growing to adulthood.

An orb-weaving spider creates a protective egg case from its silk.

Some caterpillars make waterproof tents where they live. Another type of caterpillar, the silkworm, spins a cocoon that humans use to make very fine fabric for clothing, which is also called silk. Caddis fly larvae, called caddisworms, build portable, underwater homes out of silk.

Spinning Silk

A spider's body has special glands that produce liquid silk. This substance looks similar to the clear or "white" part of a raw egg. The liquid is released from the rear end of the spider's body through tiny openings called spinnerets. A spider pulls the liquid silk from these openings with special claws and tiny sawtooth hairs at the end of each of its legs. When the liquid silk is pulled, this amazing material hardens into the threads we see in a spider's web.

Although it may be hard to believe, some of the delicate-looking threads of silk that a spider makes are actually stronger than steel! Thin strands of silk are not, of course, stronger than the large steel rods or beams that support buildings, but they are stronger than steel threads of the same diameter.

A close-up view of silk emerging from the spinnerets of a garden spider.

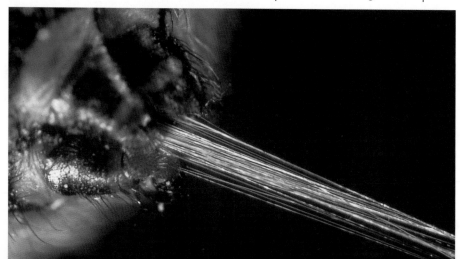

BALLOONING ON SILK

During the spring and fall, many young spiders in search of food use their silk to fly away from the places where they were born. These baby spiders, called spiderlings, climb to the top of tall pieces of grass, fence posts, or other high objects. There, they begin spinning thin strands of silk. Gentle breezes often help pull the silk from the little animals' spinnerets. Soon, long, thin strands of silk float in the air behind the baby spiders. Because the tiny spiderlings are so light, they are soon lifted into the air by the floating strands of silk. Off they go, riding the wind at the ends of silk threads. Traveling in this way is called ballooning, or gossamer flight.

If the breeze slows down, the little fliers make their silk threads longer to help keep themselves airborne. If the breeze increases, the spiderlings shorten the silk strands and rely on the faster-moving air to keep them aloft. When they are ready to land, the travelers slowly wind in the silk, making their flowing strands shorter and shorter. When there is not enough thread to keep them riding the breezes, they come back down to earth.

Where these tiny animals will land, no one knows—not even the spiderlings. Some of them fly only a few hundred yards before landing; others travel great distances, even across oceans to foreign lands! Sailors have found these animals aboard ships far from land. Ballooning spiders have even been caught in special traps on airplanes, flying more than 5 miles (8 kilometers) above Earth. Because of ballooning, there are spiders throughout the world, living in places they could never have reached by walking.

An insect's silk does not come from spinnerets at the rear of its body. Instead, it flows from a tiny spinneret, or gland, located at the head of its body, sometimes on the animal's lower lip. An insect moves its head back and forth and hooks the strand with its legs to pull it along and lay it in place.

Spider Builders

Spiders are masters of building with silk. They use it to build traps, homes with doors, and underwater homes. Young spiders may even travel thousands of miles away from home on silk threads.

Most spiders can produce six different kinds of silk—each used for a different job. A web is usually made with sticky threads, but the builder may also lay down silk that is not sticky so it can travel on the web without getting stuck. These two kinds of silk are produced in two separate glands. A female spider may use a third kind of silk to wrap and protect the eggs she lays.

Underground Homes

Most people have seen the spider webs that hang above the ground, designed to capture unsuspecting insects. Few, however, have seen the underground tunnels where some spiders live. Many of these underground homes have doors of silk that cover their entrances. Behind these doors, spiders spend most of their lives—resting, eating, and raising their young in safety.

These tunnel builders, known as trap-door spiders, are born with special tools that allow them to work under ground. The tip of a trap-door spider's jaw is lined with rake-like spines, which are helpful in digging and packing soil. The jaws of spiders that live above ground usually do not have this spiny edge.

A trap-door spider builds its burrow by first cutting a hole into the soil with its rake-like jaws. It then carries the loosened soil out of the tunnel. To prevent the sides from caving in, the spider uses its broad jaws to pack the dirt firmly into the walls. Next, the builder covers the walls with a mixture of sticky saliva and dirt, which makes the walls strong and waterproof. Then, the spider lines the walls of its home with soft silk.

When the burrow is about 2 inches (5 centimeters) deep, the spider covers the entrance with a silk door. This "trap-door" both covers the home and gives the spider its name.

To construct the trapdoor, a trap-door spider carries a load of soil to the top of its burrow. The builder then unloads the soil along the edge of the entrance hole and tightly packs it into place. Then the spider turns around and adds silk to the newly packed soil. More soil and silk are added across the entrance hole until the opening is entirely covered. The spider then attaches a small piece of silk to both the covering and the wall to make a hinge for the trapdoor.

A female trap-door spider emerges from her burrow.

When the trapdoor is finished, the top is usually level with the surface of the ground. The builder camouflages (disguises) the door with soil and small plants, making it almost impossible to see. Behind this trapdoor, the spider can live protected from the hot sun, cold wind, pouring rain, and many enemies.

The California trap-door spider

The California trap-door spider builds one of the best-known tunnel homes in the world. This vertical, tube-shaped burrow is about 1 inch (2.5 centimeters) wide and 5 to 8 inches (13 to 20 centimeters) deep. The trapdoor that covers the spider's burrow is very thick, well camouflaged, and fits tightly in the opening of the tunnel. This spider, however, takes no chances.

It spends much of its time holding the door closed. By locking its strong jaws into the underside of the door and bracing its legs against the tunnel walls, this spider can prevent most of its enemies from pulling the door open.

A California trap-door spider seldom leaves the safety of its snug burrow. To hunt for food, the animal sits patiently at the burrow entrance, with the door slightly open. Instead of using its eyes to hunt, this spider can determine the location of an insect by sensing vibrations in the soil. When an insect wanders too close to the door, the spider pops out, quickly grabs the insect, pulls it into the burrow, and eats it.

Two Australian trap-door spiders

One of the trap-door spiders found in Australia builds a second "room" in its home. First, it digs a vertical tube-shaped burrow into the ground. Next, about halfway into the burrow, the spider digs a short, side tunnel. Then, a trapdoor is built at the entrance of the burrow, and a second door at the entrance of the side room. If an enemy enters the burrow, the spider can run into the side tunnel and pull the door shut. The intruder will then search the main burrow, find no one at home, and most likely leave.

The brown wishbone spider lives in Australia as well. This animal digs a wishbone, or Y-shaped, burrow and lives at the bottom of the Y. One branch of the burrow is open at the top, and the other branch is covered with a thin sheet of silk. The silk is lightly covered with leaves and dirt to hide it from the spider's enemies. If a dangerous enemy enters the burrow through the open branch, the wishbone spider can quickly escape through the hidden doorway of the other branch.

Homes Above and Below Ground

Purse-web spiders got their unusual name about 200 years ago, when women carried long, slender silk money purses. The purses looked very much like this spider's silk tube homes.

Purse-web spiders spend most of their lives in their strange-looking homes, which are built partly under ground and partly above ground. Hidden within its tube, a purse-web spider rests, eats, raises its young, and even hunts for its food.

An American purse-web spider begins building by digging a shallow hole in the soil—usually at the base of a tree or near a large rock. The spider lines the sides of the hole with silk.

To build above ground, the spider crawls 1 to 2 inches (2.5 to 5 centimeters) up a tree or rock beside the shallow burrow. The builder attaches one end of a silk thread there, then lowers itself back to the ground. After pulling the thread tight, the spider attaches the other end to the rim of the burrow. Making sure the threads are not touching anything else, the spider adds more and more silk around the rim of the burrow. In this way, the builder constructs a delicate silk tube above the silk-lined underground burrow.

1. An American purse-web spider begins building its home by digging a shallow hole in the soil.

2. The spider lines the hole with silk.

3. To build above ground, the spider crawls 1 to 2 inches (2.5–5 cm) up a tree or rock and attaches the silk thread there. Then it lowers itself back to the ground.

The builder strengthens the tube by stretching more threads of silk between the tree or rock and the ground around the burrow. While working, the spider adds grains of sand and pieces of dirt or tree bark to the strands of silk. These materials strengthen the walls of the tube and help them blend in with the natural surroundings. The spider can now live inside its well-camouflaged home, hidden and protected from predators. Even though the outside is rough and dirty looking, the walls inside are covered with smooth, soft, white silk.

As the purse-web spider grows, it enlarges its home above and below the ground. It removes soil from the floor of the burrow to deepen the hole. The spider then adds this soil to the silk strands as it extends the tube above the ground. If it has dug up more soil than it needs, a purse-web builder simply cuts a slit in the silk wall and pushes the excess dirt out. Then, the slit is repaired with fresh silk and soil.

4. Working its way up, the spider adds more silk (from the inside)—and forms a tube.

5. The builder strengthens the tube by adding pieces of dirt or bark. This also helps it blend in with the surroundings.

HOME HUNTING

A purse-web spider seldom, if ever, leaves the safety of its silk tube—even to hunt for food. Instead, the spider captures insects from the comfort of its home.

The silk threads between the burrow and the nearby tree or rock are tightly strung, so any small movement will cause the tube to shake, or vibrate. These vibrations signal the spider that an insect is on its tube and also lets the spider know exactly where the insect is located.

The spider begins its hunt, moving along the inside of the tube until it is in position, with the insect within reach on the other side of the silk wall. The hunter then quickly thrusts its two fangs through the wall and injects poison into the surprised insect. When its prey is dead, the spider releases its hold with one fang and tears a slit in the tube. The prey is pulled through the slit and carried into the underground burrow. Often, the spider mends the slit in the tube immediately, but some spiders wait until later to finish the repairs.

Each time the tube is made larger, the spider attaches new silk threads to the nearby tree or rock for support. When the old supports are no longer needed, the spider removes them without ever leaving the safety of its home. Working from inside, it cuts a slit in the wall of the tube and removes the old lines. The slit is then quickly repaired. Soon, it is impossible to tell where the old tube ends and the new addition begins.

Full-grown American purse-web spiders build homes that are usually from 9 to 20 inches (24 to 50 centimeters) long, measuring from the bottom of the burrow to the top of the tube. Most of these animals, however, build homes that are slightly more than 12 inches (31 centimeters) long. More than half of the total length is above ground. For this little builder, which seldom grows to be more than 1 inch (2.5 centimeters) in length, its home is a grand silk palace.

Underwater Homes

More than 30,000 kinds of spiders are known to live in the world today, but only one—the European water spider—builds its home underwater. This spider spends almost its entire life below the surface of ponds, lakes, and slow-moving streams throughout Europe and Asia.

Like all spiders, the European water spider breathes air. To live underwater, this spider must carry its own air supply wherever it goes. To get air, the spider goes to the surface, turns upside down, and pushes its abdomen (rear of its body) out of the water. A thin layer of air is trapped in the hairs that cover the spider's abdomen. When the animal dives back underwater, this layer of air forms a large bubble around its body. The spider now has enough air to breathe for about one day! When the supply gets low, the spider simply returns to the surface to get more air.

To prepare to build its home, a water spider spins a thread of silk from the stem of one water plant to the stem of another plant and back again. As the spider continues to work, the threads form a small, flat sheet of silk. The builder attaches threads to nearby plants to give the sheet extra support.

Here, a water spider deposits air bubbles from its abdomen into a silk holding net.

An air bubble is trapped inside a silken net as a diving spider creates a second bubble around its abdomen.

Then, the spider begins to make its underwater home dry. It climbs under the silk sheet and pushes off most of the air bubble that covers its abdomen. As the air bubble floats upward, it is trapped beneath the sheet of silk, causing the sheet to rise slightly. Now, the flat sheet has a slight hump near the center of its surface.

The spider then goes to the surface of the water, flips over, and traps more air in the hairs around its abdomen. The spider pulls itself down the silk lines that it has spun between the surface of the water and the building site. It releases another air bubble beneath the silk sheet. The second bubble combines with the first one to make a larger bump in the sheet. As the spider adds more air bubbles, the silk sheet is pushed into the shape of a dome.

The European water spider lives in the large air bubble beneath the roof of silk. This delicate little home is only about 1 inch (2.5 centimeters) in diameter. Here, in its underwater world, the spider eats, sleeps, and mates.

A two-room bubble

When it is time to raise her young, the female European water spider builds a home with two rooms instead of one. Her home is built in the same way as a one-room, dome-shaped house, but the mother spider does a little extra work. Just below the roof, she weaves a silk floor to divide the space into an upper and lower room, or chamber. She lays her eggs in the upper chamber, and then seals it off from the rest of the house.

Soon after the eggs hatch, the baby spiderlings gnaw through the floor of the nursery and leave their mother's house. These tiny animals, in need of a home, often live inside empty snail shells at the bottom of the pond, lake, or stream. Before moving in, however, the spiderlings must carry a supply of life-giving air from the surface of the water to their new shell homes. When they become adults, the spiders will build their own silk, air-bubble homes.

CHAPTER

Traps That Spiders Build

Spiders build webs as traps to catch their food. Most people have seen a spider's web—a cobweb in the corner of a room or a net-like web between the twigs of a tree. These are the two types of webs that we see most often, but spiders build many other kinds of webs. Some of these fascinating webs look like funnels, ladders, and bowls.

Cobwebs

Cobwebs are among the most commonly seen traps that spiders build. They are found in old sheds, abandoned buildings, and even in well-kept homes. More than 2,500 different kinds of spiders make this type of web. These cobweb builders, which are usually very small in size, can be found all over the world.

Even though a cobweb often looks messy and disorganized, the webs are very well planned. For example, the common European spider builds a large, tent-like cobweb that hangs beneath the branches of a low plant. It attaches nonsticky silk threads to one another and to the nearby plant. As more and more threads are added in many different directions, the cobweb slowly takes shape. The spider then stretches sticky silk lines from the "tent" to the ground below. Soon, the prey is captured with these tightly stretched lines.

A grasshopper struggles in a web as a garden spider rushes in for the capture.

The European spider's cobweb is well designed for capturing crawling insects. If an insect accidentally touches one or two of the web's sticky lines, it struggles to get itself free. This struggling causes the tightly stretched line to break away from the ground. The line quickly contracts, like a stretched rubber band that is suddenly released. The insect is pulled off the ground and hangs on the line, until the spider pulls it into the web and eats it.

SILK LIFELINES

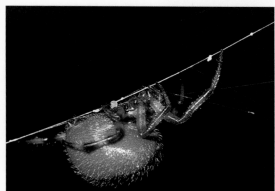

A shamrock orb weaver spider travels across a bridge of silk.

When traveling from one place to another, almost every spider marks its path with a line of silk. This line, called a dragline or safety line, is made of dry, non-sticky silk. Every now and then, however, the spider anchors the line in place with a strand of sticky silk.

When a spider is walking along a branch or sitting on its web high above the ground, the anchored thread acts as a safety line. If the spider slips or is blown by a gust of wind, the line stops the animal's fall—possibly preventing its death on rocks or in water far below. Instead, the spider dangles unharmed in the air until it can quickly and easily climb back up the line. The dragline is so important to a spider that it is sometimes called a lifeline.

Sometimes, a spider will use its dragline to escape from an enemy. When threatened by a hungry bird or insect, the spider may avoid being eaten by jumping from the branch or twig where it was standing. With the silk lifeline attached to the branch, the spider falls only a short distance. If it is too dangerous to return to the branch, the spider can simply spin more silk and make the lifeline longer. It can then lower itself all the way to the ground and wait there for the danger to pass before climbing back up the line.

Spiders also use a dragline to build bridges of silk. For example, to travel from the branches of one tree to the branches of another, a spider spins a silken thread. The fine thread is carried from one tree to the other on a breeze. When the strand of silk reaches the other tree, it becomes tangled in the twigs and branches. The spider pulls the line tight and fastens it to the branch where it is standing. The spider can then crawl across the gap on its silk bridge.

Orb Webs

The spiders known as the orb-web weavers build some of the most beautiful webs in the world. These webs are what people often think of when they hear the words "spider web." More than 2,000 different kinds of spiders throughout the world build orb webs to trap their food.

Even though the many types of orb webs can look very different from one another, most of them are constructed in a similar way. For example, a female garden spider finds a strong, sturdy place above the ground to build her large web. It may be the wall of a building, or the branch or trunk of a tree. She attaches one side of her web to this support. She then crawls along twigs, branches, and leaves in search of a place to attach the other side of her web.

Orb webs come in many shapes and sizes, but all are constructed by using the same method.

Making the bridge

As the spider crawls across the space where she will build her web, she spins a thread of dry silk. When she has found a second, sturdy support, she cuts the thread and attaches it there. This bridge between the supports is the first line of her web.

Sometimes, a spider cannot crawl across the space to find the second support. While standing on the first support, the spider spins a silk thread thin enough to be carried away by gentle breezes. It can become caught on almost any solid object it touches. As the thread drifts away, a spider may occasionally tug on it to see if it has attached securely to a second support. If it has not, the spider pulls the thread back, rolls it into a ball, and eats it! This way, none of the spider's valuable silk is wasted.

The spider sends out another silk line to catch on a nearby branch. When it attaches securely, the spider pulls the line tight. She then attaches the other end of the thread to the support where she is standing. This thin silk line forms the bridge across the space where a net-like web will soon hang.

Making the Y

After the first line is attached at both ends, a web builder makes the bridge stronger. She crawls back and forth, adding more silk as she goes. On her last trip across, the spider adds a loose strand of silk, which sags just below the bridge. She crawls to the middle of the sagging line and attaches another thread. With this second thread, she lowers herself down to a strong, sturdy object below. Then, she pulls the second line and firmly attaches it to the object. By now, the spider has constructed a silk Y beneath the bridge. The center point of the Y, where the two "arms" fork, will be the center, or hub, of the web.

How an Orb Web Is Built

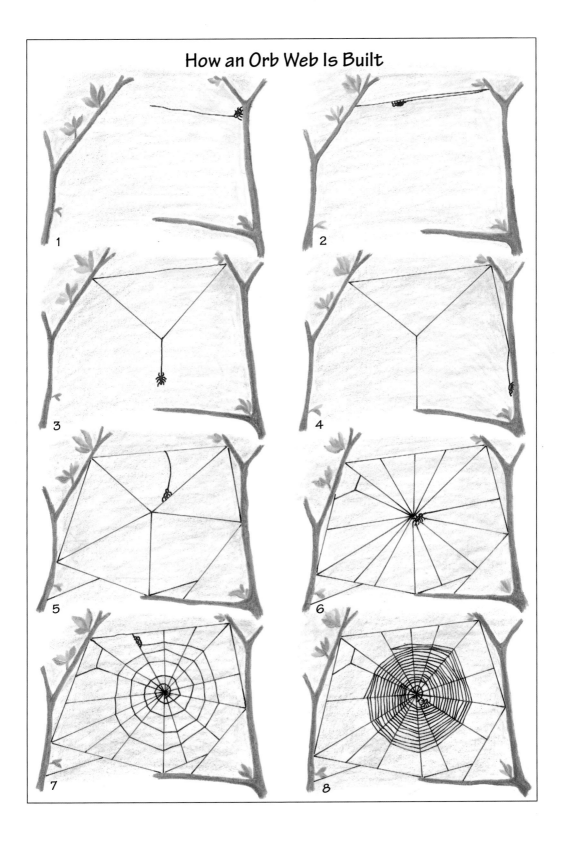

Making the rays

The spider now adds more lines from the center point to the two supports. To do this, she attaches a strand of silk at the center and climbs along one arm of the Y to the bridge. She walks a short distance along the bridge, pulls the thread tight, and attaches it to the support. One by one, she adds more and more lines of silk in this way. Soon, the web has many silk spokes, called radial lines, or rays. The rays connect the center point with the supports on all sides.

When all the rays have been added, the web looks very similar to a bicycle wheel. The number of rays depends on the type of spider that is building the web.

Adding sticky silk

The spider now moves to the center of the web, or hub, where all of the rays meet. She crawls around and around the center, spinning a thread of silk as she goes. This thread is quickly attached to each ray that she crosses. She continues around the web, farther and farther away from the hub, attaching the thread of silk. Before she reaches the outer edge of the web, she stops.

Until now, the spider has used a dry, nonsticky silk to build the web. Now, she must add the sticky lines that can trap insects. She works her way back toward the hub. As she crawls this time, however, she attaches a sticky, more tightly coiled thread to the rays. To keep from wasting silk as she goes, she eats the dry thread she attached earlier, which now helps guide her back.

Near the hub, the spider stops adding the sticky silk. The remaining spiral of dry silk is left there so that the spider does not get stuck in her own web.

Although a web of this kind looks complicated to build, most orb-web spiders can do the job in less than one hour.

Hunting on the web

Some orb-web spiders hang from the hub, head pointing downward, waiting for prey to hit the web. Other spiders sit hidden on a twig or under a leaf at the edge of the web, holding onto one of the silk lines. As soon as an insect hits the web, the spider feels the thread move and quickly rushes out to capture its prey. The spider travels across the web on the dry, nonsticky silk rays.

Webs on Water

Ray spiders attach their amazing webs to the surface of water—not still water, such as a mud puddle or pond, but water that is flowing in a stream! Amazingly, this spider builds its "web on water" quickly and easily, in just two basic steps.

First, the builder attaches three or four horizontal lines of silk to some twigs and leaves that are hanging over the stream. These strong foundation lines are often 1 to 6 inches (2.5 to 15 centimeters) long, and usually hang less than 1 1/2 inches (4 centimeters) above the water. When making the lines, the builder uses only dry, nonsticky threads of silk.

When the foundation lines are securely in place, the spider makes trap lines. To do this, the spider attaches a sticky, silk thread to one of the foundation lines and then drops straight down to the surface of the water. There, the spider attaches the other end of the sticky line to the water. Often, 5 or 6 trap lines are spaced about 1/2 to 1 inch (1 to 2.5 centimeters) apart along each foundation line.

Water Webs

1. The first horizontal strands of silk are cast out to reach a contact point.

2. A vertical support line is attached to keep the center area from dipping too low.

3. Vertical "trap" lines are dropped to the water.

This web, which resembles a comb or rake, is designed to capture insects as they move across the water's surface. An insect that touches a sticky trap line begins to struggle. Soon, it becomes caught on a second, and maybe even a third, line. The spider waits on one of the foundation lines. When it feels the tug on its web, it quickly moves in for the kill.

From start to finish, the spider can build its unusual web in just four minutes. Water webs, however, do not last long. As the water flows down the stream, its speed and depth changes constantly. Even though the changes in the water are small, they are most often great enough to break the trap lines. Some of these spiders have had to rebuild their webs as many as three times in just twenty minutes.

WHY SILK STICKS TO WATER

Little is known about the incredible "webs on water" or about the ray spiders that build them. Recently, however, both have been found around streams in the tropical forests of Central America. Scientists are working to learn more about the webs, the spiders, and the way their silk attaches to the water.

On the water's surface, molecules are pushed closely together to form a very delicate "skin." This skin is called the surface film, and some small, lightweight insects can walk on top of it. These are the animals that the ray spiders eat. Surface film is important to ray spiders for another reason, too—the spiders attach one end of each of their trap lines to this skin on the water's surface.

Sheet Webs

The tiny spiders known as the sheet-web weavers live all over the world. Their beautiful webs, often designed in unusual shapes, are easily found in bushes and tall grasses. It is sometimes best to look for them in the early morning, when the beads of dew on the silk threads make them easier to see.

Bushes and tall grasses make the ideal foundations for sheet webs.

THE BOWL-AND-DOILY SPIDER

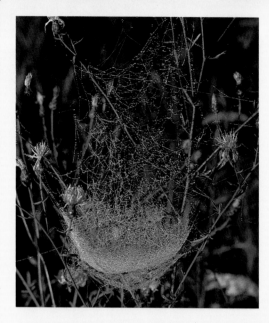

The bowl-and-doily web is a unique kind of sheet web.

Some sheet-web spiders build webs that are shaped like right-side-up bowls. One of the most interesting and unusual is the web built by the bowl-and-doily spider. Insects become trapped in the many silk lines that fill the "bowl." The spider attacks its prey from underneath the web. Between the bottom of the bowl and the ground is a sheet of silk that resembles a paper or lace doily. This lower sheet web may help protect the spider from its enemies that approach from below.

One type of sheet-web weaver builds a dome-shaped web that looks like an upside-down bowl. The top of the dome is held up by many silk lines, which are attached to twigs and branches above the web. An insect that wanders into this tangled maze of supporting lines seldom gets out. Although few sticky lines are used in this web, it is almost impossible for the insect to escape. The trapped animal constantly trips over line after line while trying to get free. As the insect stumbles about on the top surface of the dome, the spider under the dome moves toward it. When directly beneath the insect, the spider pulls its prey through the silk wall that separates them. The spider later repairs the tear in the dome.

Swinging Glueballs

Instead of building elaborate net-like webs, bolas spiders catch flying moths with one or two short threads of silk and a drop of "superglue." Their traps are named after the *bolas*, a weapon made of heavy balls attached to the ends of strong rope, which is used to catch animals in South America.

The action begins at night. The animal attaches one end of a strong, silk line under a horizontal branch. Then, it attaches the other end a short distance away. Another piece of silk, about 2 inches (5 centimeters) long, is attached to the middle of the line. The two pieces of silk form a Y-shape.

Now, the bolas spider produces a large ball of its superglue, which it attaches to the bottom of the Y. The spider is now ready to hunt flying moths with this simple but effective weapon—its own silky bolas.

Bolas spiders hunt by swinging strands of silk and hitting prey with sticky glueballs attached to the ends.

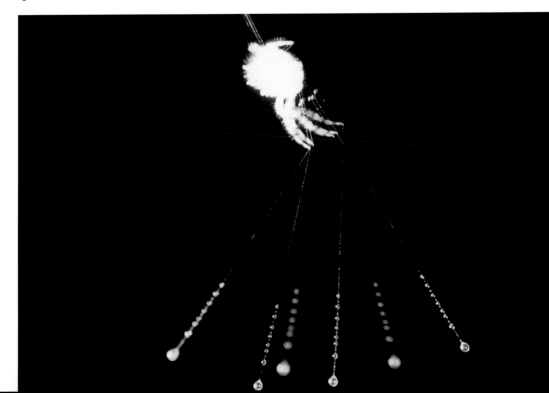

A bolas spider finishes the silk wrapping it has placed around a recently captured moth.

Using the bolas requires patience and skill. The little hunter hangs quietly beneath the tree branch, holding the strand of silk that has the ball of glue attached. As a moth approaches, the spider gets ready to attack. The hunter tricks its prey into coming close by releasing a certain odor into the air that attracts male moths. It is the same odor that female moths release when attracting a mate. Instead of finding a mate, however, the moth finds a hungry spider.

When the prey is close enough, the spider swings the ball of glue at the moth. When the superglue ball hits the insect, there is little chance for escape. The spider pulls in its fluttering catch like a fisherman pulling in a fish. The prey is often wrapped in silk for storage or transportation.

FUN WITH FUNNELS

Working close to the ground, the funnel-web spider weaves a flat, silk sheet. In the middle of the sheet, the spider leaves a small hole. It then weaves a short tube of silk below the hole, on the underside of the sheet. The funnel builder spends most of its life hidden from its enemies in this tube of silk. The spider sits so that a couple of its feet are touching the web. As soon as an insect lands on this silky, sticky sheet, the spider feels the web move and quickly rushes out of the tube to capture its prey. Then the spider takes the insect into its tube to be eaten in safety.

A grasshopper lies trapped in the sticky strands of a funnel web.

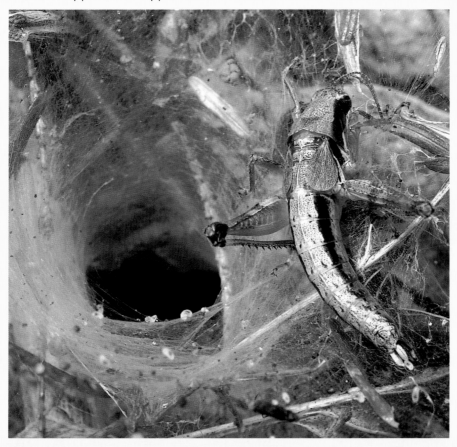

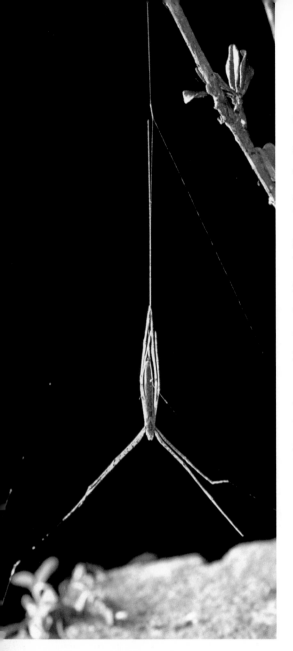

An ogre-faced spider hangs near the ground before building its trap.

"Handheld" Nets

One of the strangest webs in the world is built by the ogre-faced spider. Instead of hanging its web between the twigs of a tree, as many spiders do, this spider holds its web between four of its eight legs. This may seem like an awkward way to capture a meal, but this spider is an excellent hunter with its "handheld" net—it rarely goes hungry!

The sticky net of an ogre-faced spider is small but very complicated to construct. The spider often builds it under a horizontal branch of a bush. First, the spider constructs a frame with dry silk. While holding on to these lines with its front legs, the spider uses its hindmost legs to attach more lines to the frame.

Then, the ogre-faced spider begins to build its trap with a very sticky kind of silk that is both strong and elastic. The spider weaves several of these lines into a small rectangle about the size of a postage stamp. Next, it moves its body from one side of the rectangle to the other, filling the area with more sticky silk. Soon, it has built a very strong, sticky net. The builder then turns around on the dry frame and grabs the net with its four front feet. Each foot holds a separate corner of the net.

The spider hangs upside down, holding onto the dry frame with its four hind feet. Holding the sticky part of the web close to its body, the ogre-faced hunter is now ready to capture a meal.

When an insect comes too close, the spider stretches its four front legs out and lowers the net toward the insect. While pushing the net downward, it also spreads its four front legs apart, making the web bigger. As the insect tries to escape, it becomes trapped in the sticky silk net. The spider then rolls the net up around the insect and eats both.

The ogre-faced spider only hunts at night. If it does not catch an insect during the night, it rolls up the net in the morning and eats it, so that the valuable silk is not wasted. For the rest of the day, it hides from its enemies in nearby plants.

The ogre-faced spider trap is a tiny box made from strands of sticky silk.

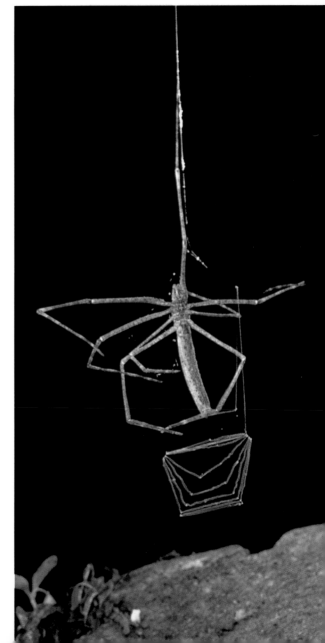

Triangle Webs

Another kind of "handheld" web is built by the triangle spider. Its web looks like a small, triangular section of an orb web (page 27). This spider uses only four rays to make its web. They are connected to one another at one side of the web. From here, a line of silk is attached to a sturdy support. Threads of silk are laid across the rays to make this triangle-shaped trap.

To catch its prey, a triangle spider crawls out to the line of silk where the four rays meet. There, the spider stretches out, with its head facing the web. While holding the line with its back legs, the spider pulls the strands tight with its front legs. Because the spider has released the tension in that section of the line, a loop of silk now sags beneath the animal. When an insect flies into the sticky web, the hunter releases the line it is holding. The change in tension causes the web to spring forward. The struggling insect becomes entangled in even more sticky lines of silk. The triangle spider has caught its meal.

How a Triangle Web Is Built

Silk Ladders

Spiders that build ladders of silk work only at night. Their webs are built each evening after the sun goes down and are completely destroyed before morning.

Scientists have discovered two different kinds of ladder webs. Both are long, narrow traps with an orb-type web at one end. One web has the orb at the top of the ladder; the other has the orb at the bottom.

These spiders build their unusual webs, which may be more than 3 feet (1 meter) long and more than 6 inches (15 centimeters) wide, to capture moths. Most spider webs cannot capture moths because the insect's wings have special scales that are loosely attached. When a moth flies into a sticky spider web, its wing scales come off on the tiny drops of glue that cover the threads of silk. Soon, the glue is covered with scales and is no longer sticky. The moth is now able to escape the trap.

To escape from a long, ladder web, a moth tries to fly up over the top of the web or down under it. Each time the insect hits the sticky silk threads, more of its wing scales are removed. Before the moth can escape from the long ladder, the insect has most often lost all its protection against the glue. Soon, the moth is trapped and the ladder spider has captured another meal.

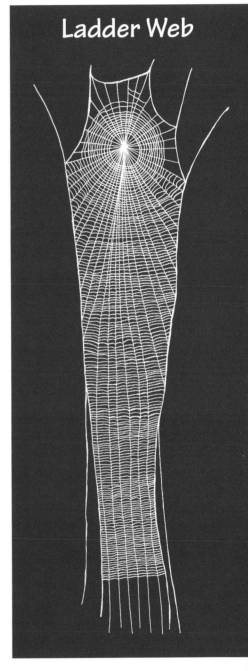

Ladder Web

Caterpillar Builders

When it comes to building with silk, caterpillars are wonderful architects. The tent caterpillar, for example, works with its brothers and sisters to construct a large, thick tent. The money-making silkworm is prized by the people of China for its silk cocoon, which is used to make fine, expensive fabric. Bagworm caterpillars build camouflaged silk homes that they carry with them wherever they go.

MORPHING MADNESS

Moths and butterflies are some of the most beautiful insects in the world, but they do not begin their lives that way. Before they have wings and can fly, these animals crawl from place to place, like worms, eating plants and growing larger and stronger. During this early stage of their lives, they are caterpillars. As they develop to adulthood, they change their form.

This change from one kind of body into another very different kind of body is called metamorphosis. For insects, metamorphosis can be either incomplete or complete. Incomplete metamorphosis is when an insect hatches from an egg and looks similar to its parents, only smaller. Grasshoppers, for example, undergo incomplete metamorphosis.

An insect that goes through complete metamorphosis—such as a butterfly—develops in four stages: egg, larva, pupa, adult. When the egg hatches, a worm-like larva emerges. During this stage, the larva eats large amounts of food and grows very fast. At the end of this rapid growth stage, the insect becomes a pupa. The pupa remains motionless and appears to be dead, but it is not. Under the body cover that we can see, the insect is still changing. When these changes are complete, the adult insect emerges.

Silk Tents

In the world of caterpillars, the tentmakers are unusual. Most of their relatives are loners, spending their lives without the company of other caterpillars. Tent caterpillars, however, live together in small groups called colonies. Each tent caterpillar depends on the other members of its group to survive.

Eggs that produce tent caterpillars are laid in a wide band around the branch of a tree. When the eggs hatch, each animal produces a very thin strand of liquid silk from a spinneret located on its lower lip. The strands harden into strong threads when they come into contact with air. Wherever these animals go, the silk liquid continues to flow. Tentmakers produce silk throughout most of their lives as caterpillars.

A tent caterpillar nest usually begins where branches fork off into many different directions.

A newly hatched tent caterpillar uses its silk as a safety line. As the baby caterpillar crawls along slippery twigs and leaves, it steadily lays down an almost invisible thread of silk. The small animal holds on to the silk line with tiny claws on its feet. This thin, silk line can prevent slipping and falling, but it helps the caterpillar in another very important way. It helps to keep the young insect from getting lost. By simply turning around and following the thread back to where it began, the caterpillar can always return home.

When all of the tent caterpillars emerge from their eggs, the colony begins building a silk tent in which to live. First, they find a place to build their home. The colony builds its tent in a tree, usually in the area where a limb forks into several smaller branches.

As they start to work, the builders also start eating. After feeding on whatever tender leaves they can find nearby, the members of the colony return to the fork in the tree to rest. As they wander around the forked branches, they leave fine silk threads wherever they go. Eventually, these threads form a silk pad upon which the caterpillars rest for the night. This pad soon becomes the floor of their home.

Next, the caterpillars add the framework for the walls and roof of the tent. They lay short threads from the tree's branches to their silk floor. Gradually, more and more lines are added. Some stretch from nearby branches to the silk floor. Other lines are attached between the branches and between the lines themselves. When the work is done, the tent has a sturdy framework.

Finishing the Tent

To complete their home, the tentmakers wander back and forth across the foundation lines, adding silk as they go. The finished tent is large enough for a colony of about 200 builders, each only 1/4 inch (6 millimeters) long, that huddle together inside for protection.

When they are hungry, the members of the colony follow familiar highways of silk leading out of their home onto branches full of leaves. Gradually, the highways get larger and thicker as the hungry caterpillars travel along them several times a day, laying thin strands of silk each time.

As the caterpillars crawl on the tent and the branches around it, more silk is added there, too. The simple, one-room tent soon gets larger and larger. Eventually, it measures several feet across and has many rooms inside. As the sun provides heat, rooms on the sunny side of the tent will be quite warm; those rooms on the shady side will be cooler.

Toward the end of the caterpillars' life cycle, their tent becomes brown and heavy with the colony's wastes.

As fragile as a silk home may seem, it is really very sturdy and protects the colony in many ways. The caterpillars can live safely inside their tent even when the weather conditions outside could kill them. For example, these animals would die if forced to live too long in very dry or very damp air. When the air is dry, the tent holds moisture. When it rains, the caterpillars remain dry, because the tent's silk walls are waterproof. The tent even protects the animals from wind.

As time passes, what began as a beautiful silky white palace slowly becomes a dirty, brown mass. The change is caused by the bodies of caterpillars that did not survive, and by waste products that the colony drops within its home. Soon, however, the tent caterpillars will be changing into moths and leaving their messy house behind.

Money-Making Cocoons

Some of the most famous, and maybe the most appreciated, insects are called silkworms. These insects produce most of the silk used in fabrics today. Even though several different kinds of silkworms are found throughout the world, the most important is the one known to scientists as *Bombyx mori*.

The threads of silk produced by this silkworm were used in China about 4,000 years ago to make the first silk fabric. Soon, the Chinese began collecting silkworms throughout the country to make this beautiful fabric. Eventually, fewer and fewer of these silkworms were left in the wild. As a result, for many centuries, almost all silkworms have been raised in captivity. Producing silk by raising silkworms, through all stages of development, is called sericulture.

A silkworm begins its life inside a tiny, gray egg. When it is ready to hatch, the animal uses its sharp jaws to cut the egg open. A small, white caterpillar, about 1/12 inch (2 millimeters) long, is born. This newborn silkworm grows rapidly, eating mainly the leaves of mulberry trees. Although they can eat other foods, such as lettuce or strawberry plant leaves, *Bombyx* makes its best silk when fed mulberry leaves. In fact, the scientific name for these caterpillars, *Bombyx mori*, means "silkworm of the mulberry."

Five to six weeks after hatching, the caterpillar is 3 1/2 to 4 inches (9 to 10 centimeters) long and fully grown. The animal becomes restless and begins looking around for a place to build its cocoon. Silkworms raised in captivity are provided with bundles of straw or twigs. The caterpillar climbs into the bundles and looks for a good building site. Then, *Bombyx* begins

The Bombyx mori silkworm spins a cocoon of fine silk around itself.

attaching lines of silk to the nearby twigs or straws. When the animal has finished, the lines look similar to a cobweb and form a safety net around the builder.

The silkworm now begins building a protective cocoon around its body, using a thin strand of silk that flows from a spinneret on its lower lip. As one gland produces this silk, another gland produces a sticky, glue-like substance that covers the silk. As the liquid silk flows from the spinneret and reacts with the air, it immediately hardens into a thin, smooth strand.

By moving its head in a twisting motion, the silkworm slowly winds the silk around its body. *Bombyx mori* can build its cocoon in three days. When finished, the caterpillar will have made about 300,000 spirals with its head and it will have spun 1 1/2 miles (2,500 meters) of a smooth, unbroken silk thread—without a single kink—into its cocoon!

Within the walls of its silk case, the caterpillar's body changes. In less than one month, a cream-colored moth with faint brown lines across its wings crawls from the cocoon. As an adult, this animal never eats and only lives for a few days.

Above: A silk moth larva lies encased in its completed cocoon.
Below: A Chinese silk moth emerges from its cocoon.

During this time, however, the males and females mate. Each female moth lays between 300 and 450 tiny eggs. Soon afterward, the female dies, but the eggs she laid are the beginning of another generation of silkworms.

Unfortunately for most silkworms, the special care they receive while being raised does not last forever. Most of them will never become moths. The silk in their cocoons is needed to make valuable silk threads and fabrics. If the moth is allowed to leave its cocoon, the single strand of silk breaks and becomes useless. Therefore, the builders are destroyed before they reach adulthood, and their cocoons are unwound to make silk thread.

In the hundreds of years since silk was first used for fabric, chemists have not been able to produce a clothing material of as high a quality as the silk these caterpillars make. When a clothing label reads "100 percent silk," chances are good that the *Bombyx* caterpillars made the threads in the fabric.

A silkworm larva travels across plastic structures designed to hold eggs and casings for later commercial use.

SORTING SILKEN STRANDS

Valuable silk thread is obtained from a silkworm's cocoon in three basic steps. First, the silkworm is killed by steaming the cocoon or heating it in an oven. Then, the cocoon is soaked in warm water. This process melts the sticky coating that the silkworm added to the silk thread to glue the cocoon together. Next, a skilled worker finds the end of the single silk thread that forms the cocoon. Either the worker or a machine then unwinds the silk strand.

About 2,000 to 3,000 feet (600 to 900 meters) of usable silk thread is obtained from most cocoons. These threads are so thin that five of them, wound together, form a strand that is only as thick as a human hair. About 2,000 cocoons are needed to produce 1 pound (453 grams) of silk.

Tube Homes

Bagworm caterpillars are another group of insects that produce silk to build their sturdy protective homes, or casings. But many of their homes are not made only of silk. Some builders attach other materials to their home. One type of bagworm makes a log-cabin type house by attaching tiny sticks, side by side, to its silk foundation.

Before eating its first meal, a newborn bagworm caterpillar, or larva, begins to construct its portable, tube-like home. It produces a sticky silk from a gland near its head. The caterpillar turns its body around as the silk is being released and soon wraps itself in a silky bag. Some bagworms live in these simple, silk homes while others add building materials, such as tiny twigs, bits of leaves, or dirt, to the silk foundation. To place these materials where they are needed, the caterpillar uses the six tiny legs located at the front end of its body. When it is finished, the tube-shaped home has an opening at both ends.

Bagworm larvae hang in a large clump on a spruce tree.

The bagworm will not leave home until it changes into a moth and flies away. So, to move from place to place, the insect sticks its head and legs out of the front end of the tube and crawls about, dragging its home along. With its head sticking out of the tube, the animal is also able to gather food. Its waste products are released through the opening at the rear of the tube.

As the caterpillar grows, it slowly enlarges its tube. To do this, it adds silk and other materials along the tube's front end. The size of the finished home depends upon the size of the builder. A bagworm's portable home may be less than 1/2 inch (1 centimeter) or as much as 6 inches (15 centimeters) long.

The bagworm's home helps protect the builder in several ways. For one thing, the building materials are usually gathered nearby the cocoon. Because of this, the home blends in with its surroundings, creating camouflage that keeps the caterpillar hidden from dangerous enemies, such as hungry birds. This simple, but sturdy, home also protects the bagworm from wind, sun, rain, and other changes in the environment.

When it is time for a bagworm to change into a moth, the animal covers both ends of its tube with silk. While sealed inside this protective cocoon, amazing changes occur. When the insect emerges again, it will be a fully developed adult moth.

CHAPTER

5

Caddisworm Builders

Bagworm caterpillars have fascinating relatives known as caddisworms. When newly hatched, some caddis larvae, like the caterpillars, build portable, tube-like homes. Caddisworms, however, build their homes underwater.

Most caddisworms live in freshwater lakes, ponds, and streams in many parts of the world. Some of these insects do not require freshwater, however. They can be found living in sea water along the coasts of Australia and New Zealand.

51

Portable Homes

The caddisworm's underwater home is made with silk threads that harden on contact with water. Many of the other materials these builders use are similar to those used by their relatives, the bagworm caterpillars. Both groups of builders often add leaves, twigs, and other plant parts to their silk.

The caddisworms, however, use two types of material that their relatives don't use: tiny sand grains and pieces of gravel. A home built with these small stones is much easier to move around in water than on land. This is because the buoyancy of water makes the stones lighter.

A caddis fly larva emerges from a case made of silk and other materials, such as sticks and gravel.

When completed, a caddisworm's tube can be many times longer than its body and can incorporate a good deal of stone and silk.

The portable, tube-like homes of caddisworms have many different shapes and sizes. They may be long and narrow or short and fat. The walls of the tube may be round, square, or triangle shaped. Some of these animals' homes are straight tubes. Others are curved, and a few are coiled, like a snail shell.

Adult caddis flies live on land, even though they spend the first part of their lives under water.

When the caddis larva finishes growing, it must prepare to become an adult caddis fly. To do this, it closes the ends of its tube home with silk, forming a cocoon. It leaves a narrow slit in the silk to allow oxygen to enter. The insect changes into an adult within the cocoon, then rises to the surface of the water, and takes flight.

"Fishnets"

Some caddisworms build silk nets to trap food underwater. These netmakers often begin construction by first building their small tube homes. The tube may be pure silk or it may have sand, gravel, or bits of plants attached to the silk.

As the net-making caddisworm builds its house, it attaches the house to a rock or some other sturdy object under the water. The nets could easily be carried away by the current of the flowing water if they were not securely attached to an object that will not move.

Once the home is complete, a caddisworm begins building its "fishnet." The net may also be attached to a rock or other submerged (underwater) object. If the insect cannot find a good place to attach the net, it constructs a frame to hold it. The frame, like the tube, is built from sand, gravel, twigs, or other similar materials held together with sticky silk. Sometimes, the frame is circular in shape, but it may also be Y-shaped. The worm stretches silk lines by walking back and forth between the supports. When two lines cross, the caddisworm attaches them to each other. As more lines are added, they form a net.

It is amazing that these little animals can construct a strong, well-built net in flowing water. What is even more amazing is that they often work in the darkness of night.

Some caddisworms build silk "fishnets" underwater that trap food brought by the current.

Caddisworm nets come in many shapes and designs. Above are examples of the trumpet shape (1), the cup shape (2), and the finger shape (3).

Ten to twelve different shapes and designs of caddisworm nets have been found throughout the world. These include nets that are trumpet shaped, finger shaped, and cup shaped. Whatever the shape, the widest parts of the nets always face upstream, into the flow of water. As the water moves through these nets, tiny animals and bits of plants are trapped in the silk lines. The caddisworms then feed on their collected catches. A caddisworm is also always on the lookout for rips, tears, or other net problems. It will quickly repair any breaks in its net and remove twigs, dead plants, dirt, or other objects that clog it.

Classification Chart of Spiders, Caterpillars, and Other Silkmakers

Within the animal kingdom, all animals with similar characteristics are separated into a smaller group called a phylum. Similar animals within a phylum are next separated into even smaller groups known as classes. Then, the similar animals of a class are separated into smaller groups called orders.

The following chart provides information about the phylum, class, and order of the animals discussed in this book.

Classification	Characteristics	Examples	Number of Species
PHYLUM: Arthropoda	Segmented body (separate body divisions) with a hard covering. Appendages with joints.	Crabs, centipedes, spiders, insects	More than one million
CLASS: Arachnida	Two body parts: cephalothorax (head and chest), and abdomen. Four pairs of legs. No antennae.	Spiders, ticks, scorpions, mites	60,000
ORDER: Araneae		The spiders	30,000
CLASS: Insecta	Three body parts: head, thorax (chest), and abdomen. Three pairs of legs and usually two pairs of wings. Head has one pair of antennae.	Beetles, ants, wasps, bees, mosquitoes, butterflies	More than 750,000
ORDER: Trichoptera	Larva lives in water; adult lives on land.	The caddis flies	7,000
ORDER: Lepidoptera	Undergo complete metamorphosis.	The moths and butterflies	112,000
CLASS: Chilopoda	Body with many segments. One pair of legs on each segment.	Centipedes	3,000
CLASS: Diplopoda	Body with many segments. Two pairs of legs on each segment.	Millipedes	7,500

Common Names and Scientific Names

All plants and animals have formal Latin names. Many also have common names, or nicknames. The formal name of a plant or animal is called the scientific name, and it is the same all over the world. Common names, however, can be different from place to place and in different languages.

Common names can sometimes be confusing because different kinds of plants or different kinds of animals may have the same common name. For example, if someone told you that they saw a trap-door spider, you could not be certain whether it was the spider that builds simple tube-like homes, the one that builds wishbone-shaped burrows, or the one that builds burrows with side doors.

Shamrock spider

In the chart opposite, you will find the common name (nickname) and the scientific name (formal name) for each animal discussed in this book. Each scientific name has two parts.

The first part, called the genus, always begins with a capital letter. The genus includes the small group of animals that are similar to one another in many ways.

The second part of the scientific name, called the species, is not capitalized. The species includes animals that are exactly alike. If the exact species is not known, then the genus name is given alone.

Common Name	Scientific Name
SPIDERS	SPIDERS
Bolas spider	*Mastophora*
Bowl-and-doily spider	*Frontinella communis*
Cobweb spider	*Achaearanea riparia*
Dome-web spider	*Linyphia marginata*
European water spider	*Argyroneta aquatica*
Funnel-web spider	*Agelenopsis sp.*
Poisonous funnel-web spider	*Atrax sp.*
Garden spider	*Araneus diadematus*
Ladder-web spiders	
(with orb at top)	Unknown
(with orb at bottom)	*Scoloderus sp.*
Ogre-faced spider	*Dinopis sp.*
Purse-web spiders	
European	*Atypus affinis*
American	*Sphodros abboti and phodros rufipes*
Ray spider	*Wendilgarda sp.*
Trap-door spiders	
(simple burrow)	*Bothriocyrtum californicum*
(side door)	*Lampropodus iridiscens*
(wishbone burrow)	*Dekana sp.*
Triangle spider	*Hyptiotes sp.*
INSECTS	INSECTS
Bagworm moths	Many species
Caddis flies	Many species
Fish-net caddis fly	*Hydropsyche sp.*
Silkworm moth	*Bombyx mori*
Eastern (or American) tent caterpillar	*Malacosoma americanum*

Glossary

abdomen (AB-duh-muhn) The rear section of an arthropod.

antenna (an-TEHN-ah) (plural: antennae) The sense organs or "feelers" on the heads of animals such as insects and crabs.

arthropod (AHR-thruh-pahd) A member of the largest animal group, belonging to the phylum Arthropoda (awr-Thrahp-uh-duh). These animals have no backbones and legs with joints. Insects, spiders, and crabs are arthropods.

bolas (BOH-luh) A weapon made with two or more heavy balls attached to the ends of strong rope.

buoyant (BOY-unht) An upward force on objects in water.

burrow A hole in the ground where an animal lives, hides, and raises its young.

cocoon (kuh-KOON) A covering that protects the pupa of many insects and spiders, often made of silk.

colony A group of animals of the same kind living together.

dragline The thread of silk laid down by a spider as it travels. Also called a lifeline or safety line.

gland An organ in the body of an animal or human that stores and releases materials for use as needed. For example, your body's sweat glands release liquid onto your skin to help keep you cool.

gossamer (GAHS-uh-muhr) The very lightweight, delicate silk threads used by ballooning spiders.

hub The center of a wheel or wheel-like web where all the rays, or spokes, meet.

larva (LAHR-vah) (plural: larvae [LAHR-vye]) The worm-like insect that hatches from the egg in its first phase of life. A caterpillar is the larva of a moth or butterfly.

metamorphosis (meht-uh-MAWR-fuh-sihs) The change that an insect undergoes as it hatches from its egg and develops into an adult.

molecule The smallest particle into which any material can be divided and still have all the qualities of that material. Molecules are made of atoms. Two atoms of hydrogen and one atom of oxygen form one molecule of the material known as water.

orb A web in the shape of a circle or wheel.

phylum (FY-luhm) (plural: phyla [FY-la]) A large group of plants or animals; one of the primary divisions of the plant and animal kingdoms.

prey An animal that is hunted and eaten by another animal.

pupa (PYOO-puh) The stage after the larva stage in an insect's life—before it becomes an adult. A caterpillar in its cocoon is a pupa.

ray One of many straight lines extending out from the same point.

sericulture (SEHR-uh-kuhl-chur) The production of silk by raising silkworms.

silk A strong, shiny thread produced by animals such as spiders and caterpillars.

spiderling A baby spider.

spinneret A nozzle-like structure located at the rear of a spider or on the lip of a caterpillar, through which silk is squeezed out.

Source Notes

Burton, Maurice. *Insects and Their Relatives*. New York: Facts on File, 1984.

Dallinger, Jane. *Spiders*. Minneapolis: Lerner Publications, 1981.

Hutchins, Ross E. *Caddis Insects: Nature's Carpenter's and Stone Masons*. New York: Dodd, Mead, and Company, 1966.

Levi, W. H., and R. Levi. *Spiders and Their Kin: A Golden Nature Guide*. New York: Golden Press, 1968.

Naylor, Penelope. *The Spider World*. New York: Franklin Watts, 1973.

Oxford Scientific Films. *The Spider's Web*. New York: G. P. Putnam's Sons, 1977.

Patent, Dorothy Hinshaw. *Butterflies and Moths: How They Function*. New York: Holiday House, 1979.

Patent, Dorothy Hinshaw. *The Lives of Spiders*. New York: Holiday House, 1980.

Patent, Dorothy Hinshaw. *Spider Magic*. New York: Holiday House, 1982.

Penny, Malcolm. *Discovering Spiders*. New York: The Bookwright Press, 1986.

Victor, Joan Berg. *Tarantulas*. New York: Dodd, Mead, and Company, 1979.

Walther, Tom. *A Spider Might*. New York: Charles Scribner, 1978.

Webster, David. *Spider Watching*. New York: Julian Messner, 1984.

For More Information

Books

Clarke, Penny. Carolyn Scrace (Illustrator). *Insects & Spiders* (Worldwise). Danbury, CT: Franklin Watts, Inc., 1997.

Goor, Ron. Nancy Goor (Contributor). *Insect Metamorphosis: From Egg to Adult.* Old Tappan, NJ: Atheneum, 1990.

Owen, Oliver S. *Caterpillar to Butterfly* (Lifewatch). Minneapolis, MN: Abdo & Daughters, 1994.

Tailor, Barbara. Barbara Taylor. *Nature Watch Spiders* (Nature Watch Series). Dayton, OH: Lorenz Books, 1999.

Tesar, Jenny. *Spiders* (Our Living World). Woodbridge, CT: Blackbirch Press, 1993.

Watts, Barry. *Butterfly and Caterpillar.* Morristown, NJ: Silver Burdett Press, 1987.

Videos

National Geographic Video. *Tadpoles, Dragonflies, and the Caterpillars Big Change* (GeoKids).

National Geographic Video. *Web of Intrigue* (Young Explorers).

Web Sites

Expedition—Spiders!

Through the many facts and pictures at this unique web site by the Discovery Channel, learn how to identify many common spiders and see how their bodies work—**www. discovery. com/exp/spiders.html**

Queensland Museum.

Check out the lifestyle and habitat of spiders throughout the world, including how to identify them—**www.Qmuseum.qld.gov.au/nature/arachnids/arachnidswelcome.html**

Index

Photo Credits
Cover: (left and bottom) ©Corel Corporation, (right top and bottom) ©PhotoDisc; title page: ©PhotoDisc; pages 6, 12, 22, 25, 40: ©Corel Corporation; page 7: ©Corel Corporation, except top row right: © S. Morris/Animals Animals; pages 9, 10, 19, 31, 46, 50-54: ©Hans Pfletschinger/Peter Arnold; page 14: ©D. Fox/Animals Animals; page 23: ©R. Blythe/Animals Animals; page 24: ©Ed Reschke/Peter Arnold; page 32: ©John Lemker/Peter Arnold; page 33: ©W.F. Mantis/Animals Animals; page 34: ©B.G. Murray, Jr./Animals Animals; pages 35, 50: ©Joe McDonald/Animals Animals; pages 36, 37: ©J.A.L. Cooke/Animals Animals; page 42: ©Breck P. Kent/Animals Animals; page 44: ©Jack Wilburn/Animals Animals; page 47: (top) ©Rhodinia Fugax/Animals Animals, (bottom) ©E.R. Degginger/Animals Animals; page 48: ©Aldo Brando/Peter Arnold.

Illustration Credits
Page 8: Robert Clement Kray; pages 16, 17, 30, 38, 39, 55, 56: Trudy L. Calvert/TLC Creations; page 27: Sonja Kalter